KNOW YOUR FOOD

PROTEIN

KNOW YOUR FOOD

Protein

MICHAEL CENTORE

MASON CREST

Mason Crest
450 Parkway Drive, Suite D
Broomall, PA 19008
www.masoncrest.com

MTM Publishing, Inc.
435 West 23rd Street, #8C
New York, NY 10011
www.mtmpublishing.com

President: Valerie Tomaselli
Vice President, Book Development: Hilary Poole
Designer: Annemarie Redmond
Copyeditor: Peter Jaskowiak
Editorial Assistant: Leigh Eron

Series ISBN: 978-1-4222-3733-5
Hardback ISBN: 978-1-4222-3741-0
E-Book ISBN: 978-1-4222-8048-5

Library of Congress Cataloging-in-Publication Data
Names: Centore, Michael, 1980-
Title: Protein / by Michael Centore.
Description: Broomall, PA: Mason Crest, [2018] | Series: Know your food |
   Audience: Age 12+ | Audience: Grade 7 to 8. | Includes index.
Identifiers: LCCN 2016053139 (print) | LCCN 2017001342 (ebook) | ISBN
   9781422237410 (hardback: alk. paper) | ISBN 9781422280485 (ebook)
Subjects: LCSH: Proteins in human nutrition—Juvenile literature. |
   Proteins—Juvenile literature.
Classification: LCC TX553.P7 C36 2018 (print) | LCC TX553.P7 (ebook) | DDC
   613.2/82—dc23
LC record available at https://lccn.loc.gov/2016053139

Printed and bound in the United States of America.

First printing
9 8 7 6 5 4 3 2 1

TABLE OF CONTENTS

Key Icons to Look for:

Words to Understand: These words with their easy-to-understand definitions will increase the reader's understanding of the text, while building vocabulary skills.

Sidebars: This boxed material within the main text allows readers to build knowledge, gain insights, explore possibilities, and broaden their perspectives by weaving together additional information to provide realistic and holistic perspectives.

Educational Videos: Readers can view videos by scanning our QR codes, which will provide them with additional educational content to supplement the text. Examples include news coverage, moments in history, speeches, iconic sports moments, and much more.

Text-Dependent Questions: These questions send the reader back to the text for more careful attention to the evidence presented there.

Research Projects: Readers are pointed toward areas of further inquiry connected to each chapter. Suggestions are provided for projects that encourage deeper research and analysis.

Series Glossary of Key Terms: This back-of-the-book glossary contains terminology used throughout the series. Words found here increase the reader's ability to read and comprehend higher-level books and articles in this field.

SERIES INTRODUCTION

In the early 19th century, a book was published in France called *Physiologie du goût* (*The Physiology of Taste*), and since that time, it has never gone out of print. Its author was Jean Anthelme Brillat-Savarin. Brillat-Savarin is still considered to be one of the great food writers, and he was, to use our current lingo, arguably the first "foodie." Among other pearls, *Physiologie du goût* gave us one of the quintessential aphorisms about dining: "Tell me what you eat, and I will tell you what you are."

This concept was introduced to Americans in the 20th century by a nutritionist named Victor Lindlahr, who wrote simply, "You are what you eat." Lindlahr interpreted the saying literally: if you eat healthy food, he argued, you will become a healthy person.

But Brillat-Savarin likely had something a bit more metaphorical in mind. His work suggested that the dishes we create and consume have not only nutritional implications, but ethical, philosophical, and even political implications, too.

To be clear, Brillat-Savarin had a great deal to say on the importance of nutrition. In his writings he advised people to limit their intake of "floury and starchy substances," and for that reason he is sometimes considered to be the inventor of the low-carb diet. But Brillat-Savarin also took the idea of dining extremely seriously. He was devoted to the notion of pleasure in eating and was a fierce advocate of the importance of being a good host. In fact, he went so far as to say that anyone who doesn't make an effort to feed his guests "does not deserve to have friends." Brillat-Savarin also understood that food was at once deeply personal and extremely social. "Cooking is one of the oldest arts," he wrote, "and one that has rendered us the most important service in civic life."

Modern diners and cooks still grapple with the many implications of Brillat-Savarin's most famous statement. Certainly on a nutritional level, we understand that a diet that's low in fat and high in whole grains is a key to healthy living. This is no minor issue. Unless our current course is reversed, today's "obesity epidemic" is poised to significantly reduce the life spans of future generations.

Meanwhile, we are becoming increasingly aware of how the decisions we make at supermarkets can ripple outward, impacting our neighborhoods, nations, and the earth as a whole. Increasing numbers of us are demanding organically produced foods and ethically sourced ingredients. Some shoppers reject products that contain artificial ingredients like trans fats or high-fructose corn syrup. Some adopt gluten-free or vegan diets, while others "go Paleo" in the hopes of returning to a more "natural" way of eating. A simple trip to the supermarket can begin to feel like a personality test—the implicit question is not only "what does a *healthy* person eat?," but also "what does a *good* person eat?"

The Know Your Food series introduces students to these complex issues by looking at the various components that make up our meals: carbohydrates, fats, proteins, vitamins, and so on. Each volume focuses on one component and explains its function in our bodies, how it gets into food, how it changes when cooked, and what happens when we consume too much or too little. The volumes also look at food production—for example, how did the food dye called Red No. 2 end up in our food, and why was it taken out? What are genetically modified organisms, and are they safe or not? Along the way, the volumes also explore different diets, such as low-carb, low-fat, vegetarian, and gluten-free, going beyond the hype to examine their potential benefits and possible downsides.

Each chapter features definitions of key terms for that specific section, while a Series Glossary at the back provides an overview of words that are most important to the set overall. Chapters have Text-Dependent Questions at the end, to help students assess their comprehension of the most important material, as well as suggested Research Projects that will help them continue their exploration. Last but not least, QR codes accompany each chapter; students with cell phones or tablets can scan these codes for videos that will help bring the topics to life. (Those without devices can access the videos via an Internet browser; the addresses are included at the end of the Further Reading list.)

In the spirit of Brillat-Savarin, the volumes in this set look beyond nutrition to also consider various historical, political, and ethical aspects of food. Whether it's the key role that sugar played in the slave trade, the implications of industrial meat production in the fight against climate change, or the short-sighted political decisions that resulted in the water catastrophe in Flint, Michigan, the Know Your Food series introduces students to the ways in which a meal can be, in a real sense, much more than just a meal.

CHAPTER
1

CHEMISTRY AND CLASSIFICATION

 ## WORDS TO UNDERSTAND

amino acid: an organic molecule that is the building block of proteins.

collagen: a fibrous protein that makes up much of the body's connective tissues.

enzyme: a protein that starts or accelerates an action or process within the body.

legumes: the fruits or seeds of plants with pods, including beans, lentils, and peas.

macromolecule: a large molecule, or group of atoms bonded together, with a weight greater than a normal molecule.

monomer: a molecule that can link with other identical or similar molecules to make a polymer.

peptide bond: the chemical bond linking amino acids.

polymer: a macromolecule made up of many identical or similar units, called monomers, linked together.

polypeptide: a series of amino acids linked together in a chain.

 Everybody knows that protein exists, but a lot of people don't understand what it actually *does*. We're told that it's found in beef, fish, poultry, eggs, and dairy products like cheese, as well as vegetable sources like **legumes**

and nuts. We might grasp that consuming it has something to do with growing muscle (think about athletes with their protein powders and shakes), but we may not understand how vital it is to almost every other cell function—everything from digestion to fighting off germs to transporting important molecules throughout our bodies.

Your hair, outer skin, and fingernails are all made of the stuff; in fact, protein is the second-most plentiful substance in our bodies after water. Proteins carry the oxygen in your blood throughout your body and control the levels of sugar in your blood. With such an important place in our health and human structure, it's no wonder the word *protein* comes from the Greek *protos*, or "first."

The Basic Chemistry

A protein is a type of macromolecule called a polymer. Polymers are large molecules, or groups of atoms bonded together, made up of many repeated units. Each of these units is called a monomer. To put it another way, when several identical or similar monomers link together, they form a polymer. This is why they are often called the "building blocks" of polymers.

The building blocks of proteins are monomers called amino acids. These are organic compounds, or molecules with at least two different elements. (An example of a compound is water, which is made up of hydrogen and oxygen.) There are hundreds of different types of

EDUCATIONAL VIDEO

THE BUILDING BLOCKS OF THE BODY

Scan this code for a video about how proteins work.

LEGUMES, DRUPES, AND NUTS

Did you know a peanut is actually not a nut? Technically, it's a legume, a type of plant that has edible seeds enclosed in pods. Other legumes include chickpeas, fava beans, soybeans, and many other kinds of beans. Nuts are the seeds of nut trees. They grow inside of hard shells. Unlike legume pods, which split open easily when they are ready for harvest, nutshells must be cracked to get to the edible part inside.

Related to legumes and nuts are drupes. These are fruits that have a hard shell inside them, and inside the shell is an individual seed. Some drupe seeds we eat, like walnuts and almonds. But with other drupes, like peaches or plums, we get rid of the seed (what we might call the pit) and eat the fleshy fruit. Whichever one we're eating—legumes, nuts, or drupe seeds—we can be assured we're getting a healthy dose of protein.

Like peanuts, chickpeas are a legume.

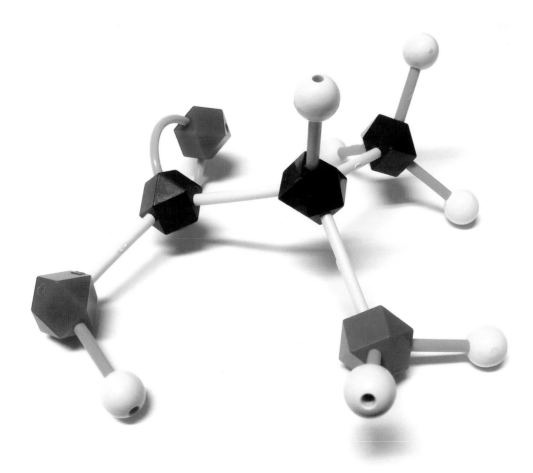

A 3-D chemical model of alanine, one of the nine nonessential amino acids used by the human body.

amino acids, but only 20 of them are used by the human body. Amino acids have specific chemical components in common, including carbon, hydrogen, oxygen, and nitrogen. Each of the 20 amino acids used by the human body has additional components—called a "side chain" or an "R group"—that give it its unique identity.

Proteins are made from anywhere from 50 to 2,000 amino acids linked together into chains. The links between the amino acids are called peptide bonds, and the chains are known as polypeptides. Even though there are only 20 base units of amino acids, they make a huge variety of proteins by combining into different sequences and chain lengths. (Think of it the way the 26 letters in our alphabet can create over a million words, each with its own meaning and usage.) After the amino acids link up, they fold and coil into three-dimensional shapes. The shape is crucial to the protein's function, since it determines what other molecules it can interact with.

Our bodies can manufacture 11 of the 20 protein-building amino acids on their own. These are known as *nonessential amino acids*, since we don't need to get them from outside sources like food. Eight of those nonessential amino acids are called *conditional*, meaning that our body can produce them but may not make enough if we are sick or stressed out. The remaining 9 of the 20 amino acids are called *essential* amino acids; our bodies can't produce these, so we need a steady supply of them from our diets.

PROTEIN CLASSIFICATION: SOURCE AND SHAPE

With all the different types of proteins to keep track of, scientists need to have ways of classifying them. The most basic classification is between animal and vegetable proteins. Animal proteins come from animal sources, like meat, fish, or dairy products. Vegetable proteins come from plants. Both animal and vegetable proteins are made of the same 20 amino acids. The difference is that plants do not consume other living things to get their amino acids, so they must manufacture all 20 on their own.

Because animal-based proteins are similar to those already found in our bodies, we can use them more efficiently than plant-based proteins. They also contain a complete balance of all nine essential amino acids. Plant-based protein sources have lower amounts of some of these amino acids. This doesn't mean they aren't good for us; it just means we need to eat a wide variety of vegetables, nuts, legumes, and other plant-based foods to get all the amino acids we need if we are not eating meat.

The combination of rice and beans is a classic way for vegetarians to get all nine essential amino acids, also known as "complete protein."

Another way of classifying proteins is by shape: fibrous or globular. Fibrous proteins resemble strands of thread or ribbon. They can bond together to form larger sheet-like structures, too. Fibrous proteins do not dissolve in water or in a variety of other solvents. They can stretch or "creep" to longer or shorter lengths, depending on the tension on either end of the fiber. An example of a fibrous protein is **collagen**, the main protein of the body's connective tissues, such as tendons (which connect muscle to bone) and ligaments (which attach bones to each other). It also gives the skin its structure and elasticity and works to replace dead skin cells. Collagen is the most abundant protein in our body, accounting for over half the total amount.

Globular proteins are the second shape. Most proteins are classified as globular. They are spherical and more complex in structure than fibrous proteins, and they are soluble in water and other solutions. They also have many more functions than

Collagen is the most abundant protein in the human body; it's vital for healthy skin, hair, and nails.

OTHER FIBROUS PROTEINS

There are other fibrous proteins in our body besides collagen. These include keratin, found in our hair, skin, and nails; and elastin, a very elastic protein that helps our skin "bounce back" to its original shape when we're poked or pinched and increases the "stretchiness" of our arteries to help blood flow.

Humans are not the only ones who need fibrous proteins. Fibroin is fibrous protein made by spiders and insects. It is found in silk and spider webs.

fibrous proteins, from storing nutrients, to transporting oxygen throughout the bloodstream, to moving molecules across cell membranes. In fact, the functions of proteins are so diverse that they form their own classification system.

CLASSIFICATION BY FUNCTION

One of the most important protein functions is catalyzing, or causing or accelerating, different actions and processes within the body. The proteins that do this are called enzymes or enzymatic proteins. They're responsible for breaking down our food into smaller particles that can be absorbed and used by the body. They also kick-start the many chemical reactions that are essential to our cells, from growing and reproducing to processing starches into energy.

Transport proteins shuttle important molecules throughout our bodies and in and out of cells. One of the most crucial transport proteins is hemoglobin, which carries oxygen from blood vessels in our lungs to all our different tissues. Another one, called serum albumin, moves fatty acids—major sources of energy—throughout our blood, as well as medications like aspirin and penicillin. Some of the other major protein functions include:

- **"Messaging" as hormones.** Protein-based hormones are molecules that send chemical signals between cells. They are like our body's messengers, constantly communicating where and how to regulate our various systems. Insulin is a hormonal protein that regulates the amount of sugar in our blood.
- **Keeping us healthy.** Proteins known as antibodies recognize and protect against bacteria and viruses, warding off disease.
- **Storing important stuff.** Storage proteins in our bodies hold onto vital minerals like iron and potassium. Amino acids in storage proteins help nourish growing embryos, human organisms in their earliest stages of development.

TOXIC PROTEINS

Considering all that proteins do to keep us healthy and functioning, it might be strange to hear that there are actually toxic proteins. Snake venom is mostly proteins and enzymes that affect prey in specific (and sometimes deadly) ways, such as attacking the muscles of the heart, causing the blood to congeal so it stops flowing, or destroying blood vessels. Ricin, a protein found in castor beans, is highly toxic and can wreck the body's ability to synthesize proteins. Eating even a handful of castor beans can lead to death. Prion proteins are in our bodies already—their main function is to protect our nerves. But if they fold incorrectly in the slightest way, they can cause deadly diseases. For example, so-called mad cow disease is caused by badly folded prions.

The deadly black mamba.

In addition to source, shape, and function, biologists classify proteins based on chemical composition: *simple proteins* contain only amino acids, *conjugate proteins* contain amino acids as well as other substances such as carbohydrates or iron, and *derived proteins* are not found in nature but are produced by the actions of heat or other chemical or physical changes. Proteins can also be classified by solubility— whether or not they can be dissolved in certain liquids like water or alcohol.

TEXT-DEPENDENT QUESTIONS

1. What are amino acids, and how are they related to proteins?
2. What are the two main shapes used to classify proteins? How do they differ?
3. Name three main functions of proteins, and provide a brief description of each.

RESEARCH PROJECT

Research five of the nine essential amino acids, including what each one does within the body, the recommended daily intake, and the best food sources for it. Write a brief synopsis of your findings for each amino acid.

CHAPTER 2

PROTEIN AND THE HUMAN BODY

 ## WORDS TO UNDERSTAND

deficiency: a lack of something, such as a particular nutrient within the diet.

edema: a condition where excess fluids collect in the tissues of the body, sometimes caused by protein deficiency.

hydrolysis: a chemical process where water is used to split apart a substance.

malnutrition: a lack of nutrients in the diet, due to food inaccessibility, not consuming enough vitamins and minerals, and other factors.

metabolism: the biological and chemical processes that are necessary for an organism to stay alive.

pepsin: a digestive enzyme that breaks down proteins into smaller molecules.

peptide: two or more amino acids bonded together.

sustainable: a practice that can be successfully maintained over a long period of time.

synthesis: the process of assembling different elements into a new material.

Now that we know a little of the basic chemistry of proteins and some of their major functions within our bodies, it's a little easier to visualize what happens when we actually *ingest* protein in its animal- or plant-based forms. Since protein is so important to our health and development, it's crucial that we get enough from a variety of different sources.

However, eating too much protein can have its own negative effects. Some people swear by high-protein diets, but many dieticians and health professionals counsel against overdoing it on animal-based proteins. For one thing, they're often high in cholesterol and saturated fats, both of which can contribute to heart disease. In brief, the key to smart protein consumption is finding healthy, quality sources like fish or unsalted nuts and incorporating them into your daily diet.

PROTEIN METABOLISM

Metabolism is the name for all the biological and chemical processes that are necessary for an organism to stay alive. These include how an organism uses food, water, and other substances to provide energy, grow, and power other reactions. Of the thousands of metabolic reactions that occur in our bodies at any given time, one of them is protein metabolism—the process of breaking down and building up proteins so we can harness their power. When we eat a steak, for example, our bodies do not just automatically use the protein; instead, it must be disassembled into its basic elements—the amino acids—so that they can reassemble into whatever new proteins we need the most.

This process begins in an obvious place: the mouth. When we chew food, we increase the surface area of each bite, changing it from a small, compact piece to a flatter, wider mass. This helps the digestive system get to work on it more quickly. Once this bite hits the stomach, powerful hydrochloric acid kills bacteria and begins to "unfold" the proteins in the food. It also triggers an

Fish dishes, like this grilled salmon, are considered healthier sources of protein than beef dishes, primarily because of the amount and types of fat they contain.

BUGGING OUT

Citing the environmental impact of factory-produced beef, chicken, and other animal protein sources, some daring foodies are going a different route: insects. That's right, crickets and grasshoppers pack a hefty amount of protein (not to mention fiber and other minerals), but they need far less water and land than cattle. They don't have to be eaten whole, either; some insects are ground up into flours and powders that can be used in baked goods and smoothies.

Supporters see insect protein as a sustainable option for feeding the growing world population in the coming decades. Detractors point out that the insects have to eat high-quality grain diets—like the kind we already feed to chickens—in order to produce significant protein. The need for high-quality grain could undercut the sustainability of insects as a widely used protein source.

Insects are a potential source of dietary protein . . . if you can get used to the idea!

enzyme called pepsin, which severs the protein's bonds, breaking it down into smaller molecules called peptides.

The rapidly changing bite then moves into the small intestine, where more digestive enzymes continue to break it down. In a process called hydrolysis, a water molecule splits the peptides into individual amino acids. With the help of sodium and potassium, the walls of the small intestine absorb these amino acids and send them out into the bloodstream and the individual cells.

EDUCATIONAL VIDEO

BEYOND MEAT

Scan this code for a video about protein sources other than meat.

Within each cell comes the final part of the process, protein synthesis, or the assembly of new proteins within a cell. This part has two key steps. The first is transcription, which is when a cell "copies" its DNA—the material that carries all our genetic information—into a new version called RNA. The RNA then attaches to a part of the cell called the ribosome. The ribosome finds a special "start" code written into the RNA, and from there it begins assembling new amino acids based on information encoded into the RNA. At the other end is a "stop" code, which signals to the ribosome that the protein is complete.

WHAT THE BODY NEEDS

The most important thing in keeping your protein metabolism running efficiently is to make sure you're getting enough. If you're eating many of the foods of the standard American diet, chances are you're OK in this regard. In fact, you may be getting too much. The Institute of Medicine suggests that 10 to 35 percent of a person's calories should come from protein, which means

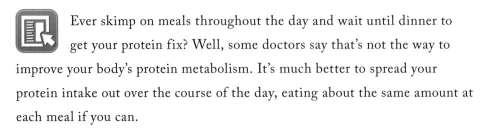

PARCELING OUT YOUR PROTEIN

Ever skimp on meals throughout the day and wait until dinner to get your protein fix? Well, some doctors say that's not the way to improve your body's protein metabolism. It's much better to spread your protein intake out over the course of the day, eating about the same amount at each meal if you can.

about 46 grams a day for women and 56 for men. (Kids 13 and under need a little less, about 34 grams.) But that's a lot less than what most Americans eat: a 2010 study from the U.S. Department of Agriculture (USDA) found that the average American male consumes 98.9 grams per day—nearly double the recommended amount.

So where does all that protein come from? It might help to imagine what different serving sizes of protein look like when matched up with different foods. There are 25 grams of protein in 3.3 ounces of ground beef, which means that one quarter-pounder (at 4 ounces) from the local fast-food joint is nearly half the recommended daily intake for the average guy. There's the same amount in two-thirds of a can of tuna, three roast turkey slices, or a couple handfuls of cashews, so it's easy to see how protein intake can add up throughout the course of a day. Some recommended serving sizes for protein are one egg, a half cup of dried beans, or 2 to 3 ounces of lean meat, poultry, or fish. Most adults need about two to three servings of these protein-rich foods a day to meet their daily needs.

Bear in mind that these recommended amounts are for people who don't exercise much. People who are out on the track, soccer field, and basketball court probably need a little more—and, in some cases, a lot more—in order to stay in peak form. (More on this in chapter four.) And even though the average

Fast-food burgers contain more protein than many of us need to consume at one sitting.

The more active you are, the more protein your body uses.

person probably consumes more than he or she needs, the fact is that protein has a lot of health benefits, including bolstering the immune system, building muscle and healthy hair and skin, and giving us more energy for longer periods of time. This last benefit is especially important for kids who are constantly on the go, from class all day to practices and homework at night. Protein is also crucial for brain function, and particularly for kids' developing brains—with so much information to process, they need the right amount of protein to keep alert and energized.

The main thing to remember in monitoring your protein intake is that it should be *quality*, not *quantity* of sources. We tend to associate protein with red meat, which is OK in moderation, but it should be balanced with plenty of other sources, like beans, nuts, and fish. A smaller portion of lean red meat and a side of black beans is much better than one larger, fattier cut in terms of getting your day's protein. Instead of reaching for high-sodium, processed lunch meats as a quick midday meal, mix your sandwich game up a bit with sardines or anchovies, which pack a lot of protein and brain-boosting omega-3 fatty acids. And never underestimate the power of soy: a half cup of cooked soybeans contains 14 grams of protein, more than other bean varieties.

Too Much or Too Little

In the same way that we need to balance quality protein sources, we also need to balance our overall protein intake. There are health risks to both too much and too little protein. Meat-based protein sources can be high in cholesterol, sodium, and saturated fats (not to mention antibiotics and growth hormones in factory-raised animals), so overconsumption of these sources can bring about a separate set of health issues.

Besides this, too much protein in the diet can stress the kidneys—whose job it is to filter protein waste products from the blood and prevent proteins from passing into the urine—and cause weight gain, since unused protein calories are stored as fat. Excess protein can flood the system with amino acids, which release toxic ammonia when they are broken down. This risks overworking and damaging the liver, the organ responsible for making toxic substances harmless to our bodies.

While there's not a ton of problems with protein deficiency in developed nations (like the United States), it can still be a problem for people who don't make healthy food choices. People on "crash diets" who severely limit their food intake are at risk for protein deficiency, as are athletes who use more protein than they consume, elderly people who don't metabolize protein as efficiently, and people bouncing back from an illness or injury who need all the strength they can get.

Some signs you might not be getting enough protein include excessive hunger; feelings of weakness; and problems with hair, skin, and nails. Since hair is 90 percent protein, not getting enough can cause it to fall out more easily. Skin may become dry and flaky because new cells can't regenerate fast enough. You're also more apt to get sick when you're protein deficient, since a well-functioning immune system is dependent on protein.

Protein and other nutrient deficiencies are far too common in developing nations, where poverty, regional conflicts, and climate change all make it difficult for people to grow or obtain food—especially protein-rich food like meat, which takes a tremendous amount of energy and land to produce. As a result, the United Nations estimates that about 795 million people worldwide are suffering from malnutrition, with the great proportion of them living in developing nations.

One type of malnutrition is called *protein-energy malnutrition* (PEM), which is a lack of protein and calories in the diet. PEM directly affects children by limiting their ability to grow. In severe cases it causes a form of rapid weight loss that can lead to death. It can also cause edema, a condition where excess fluids

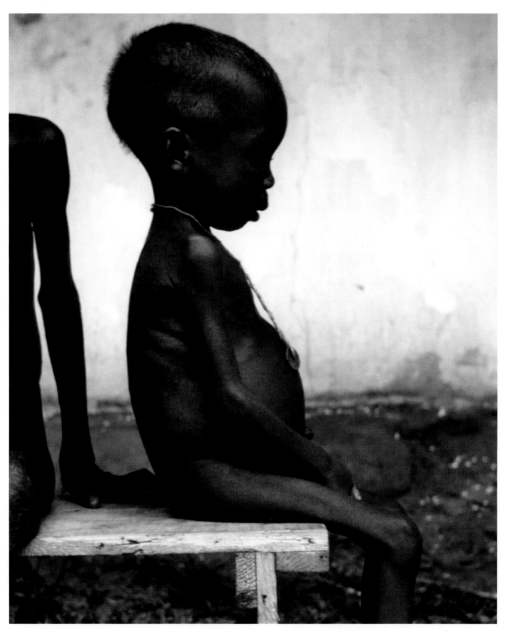

A severe lack of protein leads to a condition called kwashiorkor, which is usually only seen in parts of the world experiencing famine. The name comes from a language spoken in Ghana; it means "disease of the deposed child."

THE COST OF ANIMAL PROTEIN

 A lot of energy goes into raising animal proteins. These facts help to put it in perspective:

- It takes 2,500 gallons of water and 12 pounds of grain to produce 1 pound of beef.
- In developed nations, around 70 percent of the grain grown is used for animal feed instead of human consumption.
- Producing 2 pounds of beef requires 15 times as much land as the same amount of cereals, and 70 times as much as the same amount of vegetables.

Animal proteins are harder on the environment than many other types.

collect in the tissues of the body. When there aren't enough proteins to help keep fluids inside blood vessels, they leak out into the tissues and cause swelling.

TEXT-DEPENDENT QUESTIONS

1. What are the major steps of protein metabolism?
2. How much protein does the average American adult male need, and how much does he or she typically consume?
3. What are the health risks of consuming too much or too little protein?

RESEARCH PROJECT

Research the meat consumption of three countries from different parts of the world. Try to find out the reasons why one country might consume more than another, such as available land, climate, and more plentiful resources. How do levels of meat consumption affect the health of each country's population? Are there ways to more evenly distribute the world's nutritional resources? Write a brief report summarizing your findings.

CHAPTER 3

PROTEIN AND DIET

 ## Words to Understand

limiting amino acid: an amino acid that is lacking in a person's diet and prevents protein synthesis from operating at maximum efficiency.

nutritional profile: the nutritional makeup of given foods, including the balance of vitamins, minerals, proteins, fats, and other components.

protein complementation: the dietary practice of combining different plant-based foods to get all of the essential amino acids.

vegan: a person who does not eat meat, poultry, fish, dairy, or any products sourced from animals.

vegetarian: a person who does not eat meat, poultry, or fish.

It's good to know how much protein our bodies need to keep us up and running, as well as the dangers of getting too much or not enough of it. But in order to apply this knowledge, we've got to learn how to translate it into good dietary choices—that is, we have to learn which protein sources make the healthiest "packages" of useable protein, limited fats, low sodium, and vitamins and minerals.

It's also important to understand the best ways to balance protein sources, since overreliance on too many animal products can have negative long-term effects. On the other hand, vegetarians (and especially vegans) are at a greater risk for protein deficiency and need to assemble their diets with care; living off mac and cheese, tasty as it may be, isn't going to create a healthy and well-balanced nutritional profile.

PROTEIN COMPARISON: ANIMAL SOURCES

The quickest and easiest way to differentiate protein sources is to differentiate between animal versus vegetable, or meat- versus plant-based sources. Animal proteins are *complete proteins*, meaning they contain all nine of the essential amino acids. But they do not have as high a percentage of usable protein as some vegetable sources.

Most people's animal-based proteins come from either beef, poultry (like chicken or turkey), pork, or fish. We tend to think of beef as being the richest in protein, but that's actually not true. Red meat contains about 23 grams in a 3-ounce

Mass-producers of meats such as chicken often use antibiotics in the animals' feed.

▼▼▼▼▼▼▼▼▼▼▼▼▼▼▼▼▼▼▼▼▼▼▼▼▼▼▼▼▼

BUFFALO PROTEIN

 Bison, or buffalo, is an animal protein source that's long been overlooked in favor of beef. But that seems to be changing as people learn more about its pretty incredible nutritional value: it's higher in protein than beef, and has fewer calories, less fat, and less cholesterol than chicken—plus the added bonus of omega-3s, iron, and other nutrients. While bison may be growing in popularity, the relatively small scale of production will keep it from becoming an American staple, at least for the time being. About 125,000 cows are processed for food per day, compared to 60,000 bison for an entire year.

Bison meat is far less popular, but healthier, than beef.

▲▲▲▲▲▲▲▲▲▲▲▲▲▲▲▲▲▲▲▲▲▲▲▲▲▲▲▲▲

serving, as opposed to 27 grams in the same amount of chicken or turkey. There's also significantly more fat in beef than in poultry, especially if the poultry skin is removed. An advantage of beef is that it contains a lot of other important minerals, like zinc and iron, though these can be found in "dark-meat" poultry such as chicken legs and thighs.

One issue with both beef and poultry is an increased risk of exposure to antibiotics and hormones, which are used on many factory farms to help animals grow. (For more information on this, check out the *Organic Foods* volume in the Know Your Food series.) Pork might contain antibiotics, too, but it remains a solid source of protein. It has about the same amount as a serving of beef, with a little less cholesterol.

Pound for pound, fish might be the healthiest animal-based protein source there is. A 3-ounce serving of wild salmon has 17 grams of protein and much less cholesterol and saturated fat than beef or chicken. And the fats that fish like salmon, sardines, and tuna *do* have are actually beneficial, since they contain high amounts of omega-3 fatty acids. These are proven to help reduce the risk of stroke and heart disease. A downside of fish consumption is that some wild-caught varieties are tainted with mercury and other contaminants. There are also serious environmental concerns about overfishing and the damage the fishing industry may be doing to our oceans.

PROTEIN COMPARISON: PLANT-BASED SOURCES

With so much focus on animal-based protein sources, it's easy to forget that plant-based proteins, when properly balanced, can be a filling and healthy alternative. Plant-based sources have less cholesterol and saturated fat, lowering the risk of heart disease, cancer, high blood pressure, and obesity.

The tricky part is that few plant-based protein sources have all nine of the essential amino acids—or if they do, some are in very small amounts. This makes them *incomplete proteins*. People who depend on plant-based proteins, such as vegetarians and vegans, can be deficient in certain amino acids if they do not eat a wide variety of foods. These deficient amino acids are known as limiting amino acids because they limit the ability of protein synthesis to operate efficiently within the body.

Vegetarians have it a little easier than vegans here, since eggs, yogurt, and other dairy products are convenient go-to foods for all the essential amino acids. Soy and quinoa, a grain, are two plant sources with *all* the essential amino acids and so are classified as complete proteins.

Roasted Brussels sprouts.

Some vegetables are naturally protein rich. Broccoli has 2.5 grams of protein per cup, and a cup of cooked spinach has double that. Kale, mushrooms, and Brussels sprouts are other high-protein choices. There are "alternative" plant-based proteins that are still largely confined to health-food stores, but like buffalo meat (see sidebar), the mainstream is beginning to catch on to their nutritional properties. These include the following:

- **Hemp seeds.** These have all nine amino acids (though they're a little low in one of them, lysine). They're also high in iron, bone-building calcium, and omega-3s.

- **Chia seeds.** Derived from a plant in the mint family, these seeds are one of the best plant sources of omega-3s. In addition to their high protein content, they have a lot of fiber and zinc.

- **Spirulina.** You won't find this plant protein sprouting out of the earth—it's part of the algae family, and it's often referred to as a "superfood" because it is 70 percent protein by weight and contains almost all the amino acids. Its high cost and the fact that 30 percent of people find it difficult to tolerate keep it from being a popular alternative, though.

EDUCATIONAL VIDEO

ALGAE FARM

Scan this code for a video about how spirulina is made.

With the many health benefits of plant-based proteins come a few downsides, especially for those who depend on them exclusively. Vegetarians and vegans are more likely be deficient in vitamins and minerals found in meat, including iron, B_{12}, and sulfur. This can cut down on energy levels and weaken the immune system. Having fewer food options means needing to plan menus with care. Otherwise, people can end up repeating the same few items over and over and limiting their nutritional intake.

Eating your peanut butter on whole wheat is a way to combine different amino acids to get a complete protein.

PROTEIN COMPLEMENTATION: FACTS AND MYTHS

Protein complementation is the practice of combining different plant-based foods to obtain all of the essential amino acids. Peanuts, for example, are a good protein source, but they lack sufficient quantities of the amino acid methionine. On the other hand, they have a high amount of another amino acid, lysine. Whole grains are just the opposite: they are high in methionine but low in lysine. So when you put the two together—a tablespoon of peanut butter on a slice of whole-wheat toast, for example—you're covering your bases on both amino acids. Quick and easy combinations like rice and beans or hummus and pita bread are some other examples.

Note that protein complementation is just a dietary strategy and not a necessary practice. The idea that vegetarians have to combine plant sources at every meal to make complete proteins was once a commonly held belief, but it has since been

▼▼▼▼▼▼▼▼▼▼▼▼▼▼▼▼▼▼▼▼▼▼▼▼▼

BUCKWHEAT

 Buckwheat (sometimes called kasha), a plant related to rhubarb that is grown for its grain-like seeds, is another complete vegetable protein. Buckwheat noodles, called *soba* in Japan, are made from buckwheat flour. They're often served cold with some type of sauce, like spicy peanut sauce, and vegetables. Buckwheat is a great base for breakfast options, too—its flour can be used in pancake batter, or its seeds can be boiled into a hot porridge or baked with other seeds and natural sweeteners to make granola.

▲▲▲▲▲▲▲▲▲▲▲▲▲▲▲▲▲▲▲▲▲▲▲▲

debunked by the medical community. It's not important that we get every essential amino acid in every mouthful of food; what matters is that we get a balance of amino acids throughout the day. As long as a vegetarian's diet includes a variety of plant-based foods and contains sufficient calories, she or he is almost certain to get all the necessary essential amino acids.

KIDS AND VEGETARIANISM

For various health or ethical reasons, such as being opposed to the killing of animals, some people choose not to eat meat. Vegans eat only plant-derived foods, even avoiding things like honey that come from animals. Vegetarians have a few more options, but they still refrain from all meat, poultry, and fish. The three most common vegetarian diets are:

- **lacto-ovo:** no meat, poultry, or fish, but includes eggs and dairy.
- **lacto-vegetarian:** no meat, poultry, fish, or eggs, but includes dairy.
- **ovo-vegetarian:** no meat, poultry, fish, or dairy, but includes eggs.

Some kids choose to go vegetarian from an early age. This could be because their families are vegetarian, or maybe they're starting to understand the effects meat can have on health, or the environmental impacts of factory farms. Whatever the motivation, vegetarian diets are fine for most kids. Like adult vegetarians, they need to be sure to get a variety of grains, legumes, vegetables, nuts, and seeds in order to have a balance of amino acids, vitamins, and minerals. They also need to keep a close eye on their intake vitamin B_{12}. The good news is that many breakfast cereals are fortified with this and other nutrients. Kids on vegan diets can still be well nourished, but they'll have to make sure they're getting calcium from leafy green vegetables like kale and Swiss chard, or else from drinking fortified rice or soy milk.

TEXT-DEPENDENT QUESTIONS

1. What are some common sources of animal protein?
2. Name two vegetables that are naturally high in protein.
3. What is protein complementation, and is it a necessary practice for those on plant-based diets?

RESEARCH PROJECT

Imagine you are in charge of creating a high-protein menu for a vegetarian friend. Research plant-based protein sources that are high in different amino acids. What are the tastiest ways of preparing these ingredients so your friend gets all the essential amino acids he or she needs? Create a day's menu with breakfast, lunch, and dinner, explaining your choices and how they meet protein requirements.

PROTEIN FOR ATHLETES

WORDS TO UNDERSTAND

anabolic steroids: synthetic versions of the male hormone testosterone, used by doctors to treat certain hormonal issues in patients—but sometimes abused by athletes to "bulk up" or enhance performance.

casein protein: along with whey protein, one of the two major proteins found in milk.

glucose: a type of sugar in the blood, and one of the main energy sources for the body.

glycogen: the stored form of glucose in the liver and muscles.

human growth hormone: a substance produced by the body that stimulates growth of muscle and bone; it is sometimes used to enhance athletic performance.

sedentary: spending a lot of time sitting; generally inactive.

whey protein: along with casein protein, one of the two major proteins found in milk.

There's no doubt about it: if you're an athlete, you're going to need sufficient protein. Protein plays a key role in rebuilding and restoring muscle lost during periods of vigorous exercise. The protein enzyme called glycogenin helps turn **glucose** into **glycogen**, giving us a long-term energy supply. If stores of glycogen become too low, proteins step up and help produce extra energy so the body can continue its workout.

Proteins are involved in maintaining weight, protecting the immune system (so we can push our bodies without too much fear of getting sick), and transporting important nutrients throughout our systems so we can achieve maximum performance. By consuming enough protein, we're helping ward off the feelings of hunger and fatigue that can really slow us down.

PROTEIN POINTERS

One of the biggest myths out there about protein and sports is that simply consuming a ton of protein will help build muscle mass. It won't. In fact, overconsumption of protein can have negative effects on the body, taxing the kidneys and potentially causing dehydration or weight gain. The only surefire way to build muscle is to consume a healthy, well-balanced diet with a variety of protein sources *and* to exercise vigorously.

EDUCATIONAL VIDEO

HOW MUCH PROTEIN DO YOU NEED?

Scan this code for a video about protein requirements.

So how much protein is enough for an athlete? Daily recommendations vary based on the athlete's age, weight, training level, and type and intensity of workout. But a good general guide is about 0.5 to 1.0 grams of protein per pound of body weight. Of course, that can vary: teenage athletes fall in the 0.5 to 0.9 grams-per-pound range, while an experienced cyclist might need about 0.8 grams per pound, and a "strength and power" athlete such as an elite

Different activities may require different amounts of protein.

bodybuilder may consume well over 1.5 grams per pound. Sedentary people who spend the bulk of their day sitting need less protein than active ones.

Based on these recommendations, a 115-pound female high school swimmer would want to eat about 80 grams of protein a day (at 0.7 grams per pound), while a 160-pound male high school basketball player might need around 100 grams during peak training periods.

Of course, most of us don't have time to sit around and weigh every gram of protein we consume throughout the day. But if you keep in mind that 3 ounces of meat, fish, or poultry each have around 22 grams of protein, a slice of cheese pizza has a little over 12 grams, and a glass of milk has 8 grams, then just by mixing and matching some common food choices should enable you to hit your protein mark. But be careful—you don't want to overdo it on greasy, fast-food-style proteins, which are high in processed fats and sodium. A burger and fries may give you an initial burst of

Avocados are a healthy source of fat.

energy, but it won't last as long as whole foods like nuts or legumes, and it might even cause your energy levels to crash mid-workout.

And remember that a healthy diet is not just about protein. Athletes need to balance healthy fats and carbohydrates in their diets, too. Carbs are the most immediate sources of energy during exercise, and fats have the highest concentration of energy of all the nutrients. Try to avoid processed carbs like cakes and pastries, though. These aren't as nutrient rich as natural carbs (think whole grains, fruits, and vegetables), and they can cause unnatural spikes in blood sugar that can affect performance. Mix in some healthy fat sources like avocados, walnuts, and fish to keep your heart healthy as it powers your activity. A burger or a couple slices of pizza aren't necessarily bad, but a *diet* of them is. Just as you need to vary your activities during practice, you also need to vary your food sources when you get out of the gym.

POST-WORKOUT RESTORATION AND PROTEIN SUPPLEMENTS

In addition to *what* kinds of proteins athletes select, the timing of *when* they're eaten throughout the day can have an effect on workouts. Getting some easily digested protein, like that in yogurt, at breakfast helps replenish nutrient stores lost during sleep and gives much-needed energy for the rest of the day. About an hour or two before practice is a good time to grab a protein-rich snack like peanut butter on toast. But the most crucial moment to ingest protein comes within 30 minutes *after* your workout, when the tiny tears in your muscles are crying out to be rebuilt and restored.

The two major proteins found in milk, called **casein** and **whey** proteins, are both great for this purpose. The body digests whey protein quickly, so it can get right to work repairing muscle tissue. Casein protein digests more slowly, supplying a steady stream of amino acids to your body for several hours after your workout. To make sure you're getting both, try a post-workout smoothie made from yogurt and fruit; if you're pressed for time, a glass of chocolate milk is a quick shot of carbs and protein.

Speaking of smoothies, a quick word on protein shakes, powders, and other supplements is in order. First, remember they're called *supplements* for a reason—

ANOTHER MEASUREMENT METHOD

Some athletes base their protein intake on the percentage of total calories they're consuming. Each gram of protein provides 4 calories, and sports doctors recommend that protein account for 10 to 15 percent of the day's calories. Active teenage boys burn through about 3,000 calories a day, and girls about 2,400. This method might work for some people, but the grams-per-weight method is a little simpler to calculate and gives more individualized results.

they're meant to supplement and not regularly replace full, well-balanced meals. Here are a few of the main types:

- *Protein powders* are made from a variety of different protein sources (see sidebar), often blended with milk or yogurt and fruit to make a nutrient-rich shake.

- *Weight gainers* contain protein, but also a healthy serving of carbohydrates and fat. Athletes who need to put on some extra weight use these powders either in place of meals or between meals. Be careful, though: these can provide more calories than you need and cause stomach distress.

- *Protein bars* are the safest supplement for all ages. These can be a convenient snack on the go, and they are certainly healthier than fast food. Try to avoid bars with corn syrup, tons of sugar, or artificial flavorings, which make them more like candy bars with a shot of protein.

- *Ready-to-drink protein shakes*, sometimes called "RTDs" or "meal-replacement shakes," are premixed protein shakes. They might be easier than mixing up a shake from scratch, but they often contain sugar and other fillers.

Protein powders can be used to supplement a nutritious diet, not to replace it.

Homemade protein shakes can be made with yogurt, fruit, and other healthy ingredients.

Shakes made with protein powders and other protein supplements are strongly discouraged for kids under 18. Supplements are designed for adult use and are not regulated by the US Food and Drug Administration (FDA). When it comes to getting stronger, faster, and healthier, there is no substitute for nutrient-rich foods and plenty of exercise. If you eat a well-balanced diet, you're most likely getting all the protein you need and then some. Consuming excessive protein has dangerous side effects, including dehydration, kidney problems, and weight gain. Underweight teens may benefit from the occasional protein shake, but others should rely on whole-foods sources.

You should definitely *not* consume any supplements that mess with your hormone levels, such as human growth hormone (HGH), nor those that contain stimulants.

▼▼▼▼▼▼▼▼▼▼▼▼▼▼▼▼▼▼▼▼▼▼▼▼▼▼▼▼▼

DIY PROTEIN BARS

Protein bars can be a healthy and safe protein supplement for a midday or pre-practice snack. The problem is, they're expensive, and many of them are loaded with sugars and other additives. For the do-it-yourself home cook, a quick Google search for "homemade protein bars" reveals a whole trove of recipes—everything from no-bake banana nut protein bars to vanilla chickpea bars, or chocolate peanut butter bars. Many of these recipes include protein powder, but you can also search for bars made only from whole foods such as nut butters, honey, and seeds.

▲▲▲▲▲▲▲▲▲▲▲▲▲▲▲▲▲▲▲▲▲▲▲▲▲▲▲▲▲

Besides being illegal without a prescription, HGH can throw your natural development cycles way out of whack and lead to many long-term health issues. And as for **anabolic steroids**, forget it. In addition to being illegal without a valid prescription, these synthetic versions of the male hormone testosterone can stunt growth in teens and increase the risk of heart attack or stroke. Plus, it's always more gratifying to hit your fitness goals through your own efforts, without shortcuts.

If you want a fast, protein-packed meal on the go, the best bet is to make your own shakes using healthy, natural ingredients. Try skim milk, silken tofu, or Greek yogurt as a base, then add fresh or frozen fruit and a couple of tablespoons of nut butter, such as almond or peanut butter. Just blend it all up and drink it down. You'll know exactly what's going into your body, feel restored after practice, and won't have to worry about steroids or contaminants that are sometimes found in supplements.

TYPES OF PROTEIN SOURCES

Protein powders can be made from a variety of food sources. Basically, the process involves removing the nonprotein part of the food and dehydrating, or drying out, the remnants into a concentrated powder. The most common protein sources for powders include:

- **Whey.** This is the most popular protein powder on the market. It's one of the two major proteins found in milk. When enzymes are added to milk to make cheese, the milk separates into solid curds and watery whey. The whey protein is filtered out of the liquid and dried to make protein powder. Whey protein goes to work on the body quickly, but some people have trouble digesting it.
- **Casein.** The other major milk protein, casein is separated from the carbohydrates and fats in liquid milk before being turned into powder.
- **Egg.** Egg protein is made from dehydrated egg whites. It's got a lot of vitamins and minerals, but it can also trigger allergic reactions in some people. Also, whole eggs—yolks and all—are more nutrient rich and contain more antioxidants and omega-3s than the whites alone.
- **Soy.** This concentrated powder comes from the flour of dried soy beans. It's efficiently used by the body and helps the immune system. The downside is that it can interfere with mineral absorption and cause allergies.

Soybeans can be dried and turned into soy protein powder.

- **Rice.** It's no easy feat isolating the protein element in brown rice, but it can be done using natural enzymes. It's easy for the body to digest, though it's lacking in some important amino acids.
- **Pea.** "Powdered pea protein" is a memorable alliteration and also a good plant-based protein supplement for vegetarians and vegans. It's the closest thing to an "all-natural" supplement on the market, since the protein is separated out of split peas using only water.

TEXT-DEPENDENT QUESTIONS

1. Does consuming protein automatically build muscle mass?
2. What are the two major proteins found in milk, and do they digest at the same rate?
3. Name two types of protein supplements. How do they differ?

RESEARCH PROJECT

Imagine you are the personal nutritionist for your favorite athlete. Research his or her body weight, workout regimen, and age to figure out optimal protein needs. Design a practice-day menu that covers breakfast, a pre-workout meal, a mid-workout snack or drink, and a post-workout meal. Describe how each selection covers the athlete's protein needs.

FURTHER READING

BOOKS AND ARTICLES

Bilow, Rochelle. "This Man Ran the Entire Appalachian Trail in 46 Days. Here's What He Ate Along the Way." *Bon Appétit*, August 17, 2015. http://www.bonappetit.com/people/article/scott-jurek-ultrarunner-diet.

Estabrook, Barry. *Pig Tales: An Omnivore's Quest for Sustainable Meat*. New York: W. W. Norton, 2015.

Johansson, Katya. *Vegan High Protein Cookbook: 50 Tasty High Protein Recipes to Build Muscle FAST on a Vegan Diet*. CreateSpace Independent Publishing Platform, 2016.

"Learning About Proteins." Kids Health. http://kidshealth.org/en/kids/protein.html.

Romero, Terry Hope. *Protein Ninja: Power through Your Day with 100 Hearty Plant-Based Recipes that Pack a Protein Punch*. New York: Da Capo Lifelong Books, 2016.

Tanford, Charles, and Jacqueline Reynolds. *Nature's Robots: A History of Proteins*. Oxford: Oxford University Press, 2004.

WEBSITES

Academy of Nutrition and Dietetics

www.EatRight.org

An information-packed site with many articles about protein.

Open University: Proteins

www.open.edu/openlearn/science-maths-technology/science/biology/proteins/content-section-0

This free online course explores proteins and their uses in the human body.

TeensHealth: Food and Fitness

kidshealth.org/en/teens/food-fitness/

A collection of articles on all types of subject related to food and health.

U.S. Department of Agriculture: Choose My Plate

www.choosemyplate.gov

The Choose My Plate site has a lot of tips on nutrition and exercise, including online activity and diet trackers.

WebMD: Good Protein Sources

www.webmd.com/fitness-exercise/guide/good-protein-sources

A thorough guide to a wide variety of healthy protein sources.

EDUCATIONAL VIDEOS

Chapter One: Maya Adam. "Plant & Animal Proteins—the Building Blocks of the Body." https://www.youtube.com/watch?v=8kTP1aAUPQA.

Chapter Two: StyleCraze. "10 High-Protein Vegetarian Diet Foods by Dietician Jyoti Chabria." https://www.youtube.com/watch?v=R4LyLU_TbYo.

Chapter Three: Robert Henrikson. "Family Spirulina Algae Farm in France." https://www.youtube.com/watch?v=qfCBDyPiTS4.

Chapter Four: VincaniTV. "How Much Protein Do You Need? Nutrition for Athletes." https://www.youtube.com/watch?v=il-00pUvTTg.

SERIES GLOSSARY

amino acid: an organic molecule that is the building block of proteins.

antibody: a protein in the blood that fights off substances the body thinks are dangerous.

antioxidant: a substance that fights against free radicals, molecules in the body that can damage other cells.

biofortification: the process of improving the nutritional value of crops through breeding or genetic modification.

calories: units of energy.

caramelization: the process by which the natural sugars in foods brown when heated, creating a nutty flavor.

carbohydrates: starches, sugars, and fibers found in food; a main source of energy for the body.

carcinogen: something that causes cancer.

carnivorous: meat-eating.

cholesterol: a soft, waxy substance present in all parts of the body, including the skin, muscles, liver, and intestines.

collagen: a fibrous protein that makes up much of the body's connective tissues.

deficiency: a lack of something, such as a nutrient in one's diet.

derivative: a product that is made from another source; for example, malt comes from barley, making it a barley derivative.

diabetes: a disease in which the body's ability to produce the hormone insulin is impaired.

emulsifiers: chemicals that allow mixtures to blend.

enzyme: a protein that starts or accelerates an action or process within the body.

food additive: a product added to a food to improve flavor, appearance, nutritional value, or shelf life.

genetically modified organism (GMO): a plant or animal that has had its genetic material altered to create new characteristics.

growth hormone: a substance either naturally produced by the body or synthetically made that stimulates growth in animals or plants.

herbicide: a substance designed to kill unwanted plants, such as weeds.

ionizing radiation: a form of radiation that is used in agriculture; foods are exposed to X-rays or other sources of radiation to eliminate microorganisms and insects and make foods safer.

legume: a plant belonging to the pea family, with fruits or seeds that grow in pods.

macronutrients: nutrients required in large amounts for the health of living organisms, including proteins, fats, and carbohydrates.

malnutrition: a lack of nutrients in the diet, due to food inaccessibility, not consuming enough vitamins and minerals, and other factors.

marketing: the way companies advertise their products to consumers.

metabolism: the chemical process by which living cells produce energy.

micronutrients: nutrients required in very small amounts for the health of living organisms.

monoculture farming: the agricultural practice of growing a massive amount of a single crop, instead of smaller amounts of diverse crops.

nutritional profile: the nutritional makeup of given foods, including the balance of vitamins, minerals, proteins, fats, and other components.

obesity: a condition in which excess body fat has amassed to the point where it causes ill-health effects.

pasteurization: a process that kills microorganisms, making certain foods and drinks safer to consume.

pesticide: a substance designed to kill insects or other organisms that can cause damage to plants or animals.

processed food: food that has been refined before resale, often with additional fats, sugars, sodium, and other additives.

protein complementation: the dietary practice of combining different plant-based foods to get all of the essential amino acids.

refined: when referring to grains or flours, describing those that have been processed to remove elements of the whole grain.

savory: a spicy or salty quality in food.

subsidy: money given by the government to help industries and businesses stay competitive.

sustainable: a practice that can be successfully maintained over a long period of time.

vegan: a person who does not eat meat, poultry, fish, dairy, or other products sourced from animals.

vegetarian: a person who does not eat meat, poultry, or fish.

whole grain: grains that have been minimally processed and contain all three main parts of the grain—the bran, the germ, and the endosperm.

INDEX

INDEX

ABOUT THE AUTHOR

Michael Centore is a writer and editor. He has helped produce many titles, including memoirs, cookbooks, and educational materials, for a variety of publishers. He has authored numerous books for Mason Crest, including titles in the Major Nations in a Global World and Drug Addiction and Recovery series. His work has appeared in the *Los Angeles Review of Books, Killing the Buddha, Mockingbird,* and other print- and web-based publications. He lives in Connecticut.

PHOTO CREDITS